The Tiny, Tiny Tardigrade

by

Darren Morrissey & Karen Verrall

ISBN-13: 978-1503060548

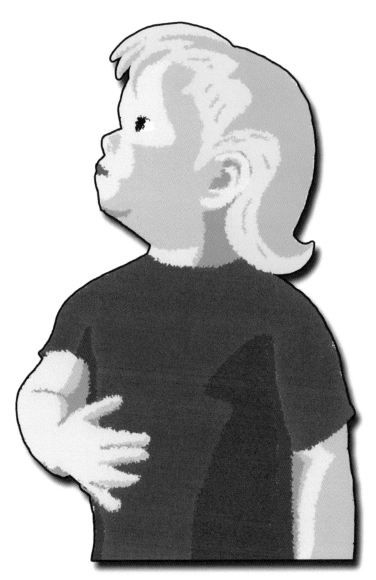

What is the tiniest animal that you can imagine?

Is it a whale?

No, a whale is huge!

Is it an elephant?

No, an elephant is very large, too!

Is it a cow?

No, a cow is still bigger than you!

Is it a cat?

No, there are lots of animals smaller than a cat!

Is it a mouse?

No, there is something smaller, still!

Is it a butterfly?

No, it is a very pretty butterfly, but even that is too big!

Is it an ant? Ants are tiny.
It must be an ant!

No, there is an animal that is even tinier
than an ant!

It's a tardigrade

Tardigrades are so tiny that you can't even see them!

Tardigrades are brilliant.

Sometimes they are called 'water bears'
or 'moss piglets'.

They like it when it is very, very cold.

And they like it when it is very, very hot.

They can live anywhere.

Even underwater.

Or in space!

Tardigrades are the second most brilliant animal in the world!

Why are they only second?

Because the most brilliant animal in the world...

...is you!

Tardigrades are awesome!

Tardigrades are about 0.5 mm long when they are fully grown. They are short and plump with four pairs of legs, each with four to eight claws also known as "disks".

They are normally found in mosses and lichens and feed on plant cells, algae, and small invertebrates. When collected, they may be viewed under a very-low-power microscope, making them accessible to students and amateur scientists.

Tardigrades are what is known as extremophiles. These are organisms that can thrive in an extreme condition that would be fatal to most life on Earth.

For example, tardigrades can withstand temperatures from above the boiling point of water, to just above absolute zero. They can cope with greater pressure than can be found in the deepest oceans and survive radiation hundreds of times higher than the lethal dose for a human, and they can withstand the vacuum of outer space.

They can go without food or water for more than 10 years, by drying out to the point where they are 3% water, only to rehydrate, forage, and reproduce when they are re-hydrated.

The Authors

Karen Verrall & Darren Morrissey

Printed in Great Britain
by Amazon